P9-DGH-052

BALLET STORIES FOR CHILDREN

by VIOLETTE VERDY

illustrated by MARCIA BROWN

SCHOLASTIC INC.

New York

Library of Congress Cataloging-in-Publication Data

Verdy, Violette, 1933-
Of swans, sugarplums and satin slippers: ballet stories for children / by Violette Verdy; illustrated by Marcia Brown.
p. cm.
Summary: The stories of six ballets, including "Swan Lake," "Sleeping Beauty," and "Firebird."
ISBN 0-590-43484-5
1. Ballets—Stories, plots, etc.—Juvenile literature.
[1. Ballets—Stories, plots, etc.] I. Brown, Marcia, ill.
II. Title.
GV1790.A1V47 1991
792.8'45-dc20 91-98
CIP
AC

12 11 10 9 8 7 6 5 4 3 2 1 1 2 3 4 5 6/9

Printed in the U.S.A. 36

First Scholastic printing, October 1991

Design by Claire Counihan

The art in this book was done
in watercolor, pastel
and pencil.

To my beloved teachers,
Rousane Sarkisian,
Victor Gsovsky, and
George Balanchine,
whose lives were the passing on
of the truth, love, and wisdom
of these eternal myths.

–V.V.

To *Margot Fonteyn,*
and the great dancers
who have made these ballets
live for us.

–M.B.

CONTENTS

The Firebird

The story of *The Firebird* is adapted from several Russian fairy tales and legends.

The title character is a wild, untamed bird—a bird on a mission. She rewards virtue, and comes to the rescue of people with enough innocence to deserve a magic boon.

But the Firebird never really belongs to anybody.

The Firebird was choreographed by Michel Fokine, and the music is by Igor Stravinsky. It was the first ballet score he wrote.

Both the score and the quality of movement are very oriental in nature, and that is one reason I loved dancing this ballet so much.

ONCE UPON A TIME there lived a prince named Ivan, who was young and handsome and brave. Now, in his land, many people whispered stories about a very special tree that grew deep in the forest. Upon its branches hung golden apples. No one who had tried to find this tree had ever returned.

Ivan decided he *must* find this magic tree.

So he went and searched through the darkest, eeriest woods until he was quite lost. Then, in the distance, he saw a golden ray shining. He crept towards it, and found himself in a mysterious garden.

And in the center of the garden stood the tree with the golden apples.

The prince had never seen a tree quite like this one. He inched forward for a better look. Just then, a flash of bright light shot through the air, very nearly blinding him. Prince Ivan held back, shielding his eyes from the brilliant glare. What could it be, he wondered?

All at once a stunning creature, made of fire, soared into the clearing. Half bird, half woman, this Firebird was indeed dazzling to behold. She had feathers of bright, bright red, which shimmered and sparkled, tapering off in fiery flames. She was magnificent in every way, majestic and proud, with gorgeous movements that seemed to whip the very air about her. The prince watched, unobserved, as she swooped and dipped towards the magical tree, intent on grabbing one of its apples.

I must capture this glorious creature, thought Ivan. He dashed forward and snapped his arms around her. Too late the bird realized the danger. She struggled in Ivan's tight grip, twisting her body in a frantic effort to free herself. The Firebird leaped at him over and over again, beating her wings, but the prince held fast.

Gradually the Firebird stopped struggling, though her body remained tense and her expression fearful as the prince circled her, examining her marvelously feathered wings and dazzling colors. The Firebird pulled as far away from him as she could.

The prince folded in the bird's wings, stilling their motion. The Firebird grew sadder and sadder in his arms, and more anxious. How could she make the prince understand that she could not live as a captive?

But Prince Ivan did understand. I cannot keep her, he decided. This is a wild creature, meant to be free.

Deliberately, he loosened his grasp.

The Firebird broke away and rose into the air.

To reward him for this gesture—for her freedom—the Firebird pulled a splendid red feather from her wing. This was a magical charm and the prince must keep it with him always. He need only brandish it in time of need, and she would be at his side.

Ivan took the feather, and bowed in gratitude. But when he raised his head, she was gone.

Suddenly he heard the sound of an approaching melody. Prince Ivan quickly hid once again. Ten young princesses danced into the clearing. They wore soft embroidered gowns and little caps. Underneath, their hair hung loose. The princesses sang and skipped, and playfully threw the golden apples in the air like balls.

How startled they were when Ivan stepped out of the shadows — an intruder! They gathered together and whispered nervously. Ivan was rather amused at their uneasiness, for certainly he meant no harm. He asked if one of the maidens might come to him.

And one did come, the most beautiful princess of all.

"Who are you," asked Ivan, "and why are you here?"

The princess was very shy, but Prince Ivan was gentle, and coaxing, and soon she was telling him about an evil magician named Kotschei. "This garden is *his* garden and everything in it belongs to *him.* Even the princesses — we are all captives of Kotschei!"

Naturally, the good Prince Ivan was horrified. He determined to do something about this evil sorcerer. Meanwhile, he and the princess were falling in love.

They danced among the circle of princesses—so happy—and when they embraced, the girls teased and pulled them apart.

But the sharp sound of trumpets ended these moments of joy. "Kotschei," they whispered. The girls, shaking with fear, fled inside the castle. The princess gave Ivan one last kiss . . . and the lovers parted.

Ivan resolved to save his princess. He, too, ran into the castle. He would finish off Kotschei once and for all! But once inside, Prince Ivan was greeted by a horrible sight. Hundreds of statues lined the cold, cheerless room—all Kotschei's victims turned to stone. Hideous monsters flew out of the shadows and surrounded the prince, imprisoning and tormenting him. But the most terrible sight of all was Kotschei!

He was a stooped, ugly old sorcerer with gnarled fingers and long, sharp nails. His body was skeletonlike, and on his head was a spiked crown of burning gold. He smiled a loathsome smile and beckoned to Ivan.

The princess pleaded for her prince, but Kotschei merely laughed, a wild and terrible sound.

At the last possible moment, Prince Ivan pulled out the Firebird's feather. He waved it in the air, and suddenly a brilliant light appeared. The Firebird! As promised, she had come to Ivan's rescue. Her very presence hypnotized the monsters. They followed her, blinded and disoriented, matching her every

movement, swirling and slinking and rising. The dance grew wilder and wilder, and the monsters leapt into the air as if, like the Firebird, they too could take flight.

Kotschei watched, furious, but unable to do anything to stop the Firebird.

Finally the monsters fell, exhausted. The Firebird floated amongst the ugly creatures, calming them, lulling them into gentle sleep. Then she motioned towards a big wooden box. Inside was a large egg, and in that egg was Kotschei's soul. The Firebird told Ivan that if he broke the egg, the sorcerer would die.

Kotschei cringed and cried. He pleaded for mercy. He tried to snatch the egg from Ivan. But the prince lifted it, and with all his strength he smashed it to the floor. Kotschei was destroyed.

The Firebird's mission was over. She rose into the air . . . then she was gone.

Morning came. The sun climbed above the trees, bathing the castle in glorious brightness. Stone statues crumbled and the humans within breathed life once again. Even the monsters had grown tame.

Prince Ivan and the princess ascended the palace steps and looked out on the newly free kingdom that now was theirs to rule forever. They pledged their love and, in that palace where gloom had reigned for so long, they were wed.

And, somehow, as Prince Ivan looked into the fiery sunrise, he knew that the Firebird was near, watching over them.

Coppélia

Coppélia or *The Girl with Enamel Eyes* premiered in 1870 at the Paris Opera, where so many of the great ballets were first danced. It was based on a tale by E.T.A. Hoffman.

Coppélia's characters are real people, not sprites. This ballet is such a natural story to dance—as natural as good country bread! It's without great adventure, but through their encounter with Dr. Coppélius, Franz and Swanilda, who start out as brats, have grown up by the end and become more understanding of others.

Dr. Coppélius is a touching, poignant character. He has a dream—to make his dolls human—that means more to him than anything else in life. When Franz and Swanilda nearly destroy this dream, and see its effect on him, they become more generous, caring people.

There is a very sad, romantic story associated with this ballet. The first girl to dance the role of Swanilda was named Giuseppina Bozacchi. She was barely fifteen years old. Only two months after the ballet opened—with France in the middle of war with Germany, and Paris under seige—young Giuseppina came down with a fever and died.

The "boy" who played Franz was actually a girl named Eugenie Fiocre!

Now, here is a story about two young lovers. The girl was Swanilda, the boy called Franz. They lived some time ago, in a cozy colorful village in a distant land. Many of the cottages had little balconies, and the streets were swept clean twice every day. It was a charming place, really, alive with spring flowers that sweetened the air.

One fine day Swanilda pranced into the village square. How pretty she looked, and how lively her step, for soon she would see her boyfriend, Franz. Looking up, she noticed a girl reading on a nearby balcony. This was Coppélia, Doctor Coppélius's daughter.

Swanilda waved. "Hello there, good morning!"

Coppélia did not answer.

So Swanilda called again, a little louder. "Hello! Hello!"

And again, no answer.

Rude girl, sniffed Swanilda. But the sound of footsteps took her mind off Coppélia. Franz was coming! "I've an idea that will be quite fun," she decided. "I shall hide, then surprise my handsome fellow with a kiss!"

Franz strode into the square, looking around for Swanilda. But, before long, someone else caught his eye. Coppélia! As long as Swanilda's not here, I'll talk to Coppélia, he thought. She's just as pretty, anyway.

"Hello!" he called, just as Swanilda had.

But this time Coppélia stood up—albeit rather shakily—and she blew kisses at Franz! He was delighted, perhaps even flattered, and he bowed a rather pompous bow. Needless to say, Swanilda, who had seen all of it, was now very jealous!

Silly lovers, neither one had noticed Doctor Coppélius kneeling behind Coppélia, orchestrating everything she did.

The moment Coppélia went inside, Swanilda burst out of her hiding place, chasing a butterfly. Franz quickly reached out and snatched it. Then he stuck a pin through the poor little thing, and fastened it to his jacket.

Swanilda was horrified. "You are dreadful!" she screamed, beating him with her fists and crying.

"I, dreadful?" Franz sounded confused.

So, mocking his voice and his bow, Swanilda said, "Hello, Coppélia." Then she imitated the girl throwing kisses at Franz. "She could not resist your charm, could she!"

"So that's what is bothering you." Franz laughed. "I was just being friendly."

"Friendly!" Swanilda threw her hands in the air. "How could you—"

"Hear ye, hear ye!" The mayor's call interrupted their argument. Villagers were gathering around to hear his announcement. "Tomorrow is a special day. The lord of the manor is giving a bell to our city. In honor of this great event," proclaimed the mayor, "all who marry on this day will receive a bag full of gold!"

Franz glanced lovingly at Swanilda. She was still sizzling though, and just glared back.

Clang! All at once the villagers turned their attention to Doctor Coppélius's house. There had been the sound of hammering, and now . . . bang! a stunningly loud explosion! Dark swirls of smoke came pouring out the window.

Coppélius ran to his balcony, fanning away the smoke. "It's nothing!" he yelled down to the curious, whispering crowd. "Go away! Mind your own business!" He dashed inside, slamming the door behind him.

"He is crazy," Swanilda laughed, "and he's got a crazy daughter, too! Coppélia doesn't talk to anyone. Except, of course, to Franz. And he is so charming with her!" Swanilda bowed in an exaggerated way, blowing kisses at the balcony.

"But I love you!" cried Franz. "It's you I want to marry!"

"Well then, perhaps you will let me test your love?" Swanilda told him of the legend of the ear of corn. "If you shake a dried ear of corn and hear it rattle, then your lover is true. But if you shake it and there is silence, your lover is false."

"All right." Franz was confident. "Let us try it."

Swanilda went first. She shook the corn. Once. Twice. She put it close to her ear and shook it again. Nothing!

"There must be a sound"—Franz gently kissed her—"because I love you."

"There is no sound!" Swanilda wailed. "No sound at all!" And giving the corn a last desperate shake, she threw it to the ground and ran off.

But when Franz picked up and shook the corn, he was sure he heard it rattle. "I hear it! Swanilda, come back!" He shook it one more time, to prove his love was true.

But Swanilda heard nothing. She was already gone.

* * *

Evening soon came and the square cleared.

Swanilda sat in her house, sulking. Even her girlfriends couldn't cheer her up, so convinced was she that Franz no longer loved her.

But Franz and his friends were more than a little spirited as they made their way home from the tavern. They were just crossing the square when they spied Doctor Coppélius stepping out of his house.

"Look!" cried one of the boys. "It's the crazy man!"

"Have you done any interesting experiments lately, Doctor?" teased Franz.

"Crazy Coppélius, Crazy Coppélius!" The boys made a ring around the old man. With shouts of laughter, they lifted him and ran around the square. In the confusion, no one noticed that Coppélius dropped his key.

It was Franz who tired of the game first. In time the others did, too, and they put the old man down. With an angry scowl, Doctor Coppélius wiped his brow, straightened his glasses, and hobbled on his way.

At that moment Swanilda stood upright, stamped her foot, and announced in a clear, determined voice that she was going to find out about this Coppélia, once and for all! Her friends were eager to help, so all in a line, rather nervous and holding hands, they inched across the square towards the doctor's door.

Something shiny on the ground caught Swanilda's eye. "Look!" She scooped up Coppélius's key. "What luck! Now we can go inside!"

Meanwhile, Franz was dragging a ladder to Coppélius's house. If Swanilda wouldn't have him, he thought stubbornly, then he would marry Coppélia instead. He had barely begun to climb when the doctor ran over and whacked him with his walking stick.

"Get away from my house!" he ordered.

Franz took off, and the minute he did, Coppélius noticed his front door slightly ajar. "I locked it. I know I locked it . . ." He scrambled into his house. "What have they done to me now?"

Now Franz came back. He was certainly determined to find Coppélia! He straightened the ladder and started again to climb.

* * *

Swanilda trembled as she entered Doctor Coppélius's workroom. The place was dark and forbidding. Ghostly shadows lurked around every corner. Perhaps this was a bad idea, after all? No! She had resolved to find Coppélia, and find her she would. So she called to her friends. In they filed, one by one.

"What's that? Who is there?" called one scared girl named Marta.

"And look there! Someone is watching us!" called another.

"Oh, that's just a doll," someone said.

Swanilda searched for Coppélia. Behind tall chairs. Under dark wood tables. Inside each cabinet. No Coppélia. Where could she be? Perhaps the balcony? She crept cautiously towards the window and peeked behind the curtain. Coppélia was there!

Swanilda tugged timidly at the girl's dress. She ran back to her friends and they all waited, knees quivering, for Coppélia to do something.

But Coppélia did nothing!

Swanilda tiptoed back. She tugged a bit harder.

Coppélia *still* did nothing!

Then Swanilda gave a push . . . and the girl slumped forward.

"She's a doll!" Swanilda shrieked with laughter. "I've been jealous of a doll!" And she walked stiffly around the room in the style of a marionette. Her friends picked up on this bit of silliness and started imitating her.

Then one girl bumped right into a doll—and it started to move! Soon, just for the fun of it, the girls wound up all the dolls in the workroom. One porcelain doll, elegantly dressed, did a stately minuet. An astronomer doll in long black robes turned circles, pointing to the sky. A boy in patchwork clothes skitted here and there, a Chinese doll leapt in the air, and a fierce warrior raised his sword to fight. In fact, his sword pricked one of the girls who got in his way! And the patchwork boy chased Marta all around! And—

"My dolls!" Doctor Coppélius charged into the room. "What have you done to my dolls!" he squealed, flinging his walking stick in the air.

The girls scattered. Swanilda hid behind the balcony curtain.

Just when Doctor Coppélius thought he had gotten rid of everyone, he saw Franz climbing in the window! Coppélius decided it was time to teach that boy a lesson. So he stood stock-still and pretended to be a doll!

Franz tiptoed around the room searching for Coppélia.

And there was funny old Coppélius, following the boy, step by step! Whenever Franz turned, Coppélius froze to look like one of the dolls. Franz thought this was very strange indeed—he even tweaked the doll's nose! Now, Doctor Coppélius did not like having his nose tweaked one bit, and he took up his walking stick at once and hit Franz, hard.

"Robber! Thief!" he screamed at the boy.

"Stop!" Franz ducked. "I haven't come to steal." Franz dodged another blow. "I've come to see Coppélia!"

"Never!"

"Please!" Franz held out his hand. "I love her."

Coppélius backed off, rubbing his chin. This boy might be just what I need, he thought. If he loves Coppélia so much, he won't mind giving up his life to her!

"Well, my boy"—he shook Franz's hand—"since you love her, I will certainly let you see Coppélia. But first, let's have a drink, shall we!" He poured two glasses of cider. And into Franz's glass he slipped some powder to make him sleep.

They downed their drinks.

"How about another?" suggested Coppélius.

"Perhaps Coppélia can join us?" Franz looked around the room. "By the way, where is she?"

"She'll be along." Coppélius filled the glasses, secretly adding more sleeping potion. They clinked a toast and drank again.

And so it went, until Franz was fast asleep.

The doctor dragged out a big, dusty book. "Now, where is that spell?" He skimmed through the yellowed pages until he found the chapter *How to Make a Doll Real,* for that was his intention: to bring Coppélia to life!

He hobbled over to the balcony, pulled apart the curtains, and wheeled in Coppélia. Only, it wasn't Coppélia who sat on the chair: it was Swanilda, dressed in Coppélia's clothes and reading Coppélia's book!

"Soon you will walk and talk and breathe," Coppélius told her. *"You will be alive and you will be mine!"*

Swanilda could hardly keep from laughing.

Coppélius scrambled over to Franz. He swirled his hands and started chanting at the sleeping boy. "The energy. All the energy. Let it go . . ." Then he moved to Swanilda and waved his hands at her. "Take the energy, Coppélia!"

Swanilda blinked her eyes and shrugged her shoulders.

"Take the energy and walk!" cried Coppélius.

If he wants me to walk, then I shall walk, thought Swanilda. So she rose with a jerky motion. She tossed away her book. Then she walked, keeping her legs stiff and unbending. When she stopped, her body trembled just a bit, as if she might lose her balance.

Meanwhile, Doctor Coppélius was running back and forth—Franz, Swanilda, Franz, Swanilda—gathering this imagined life force. Each time he threw it at Swanilda, she moved another part of her body.

Then Swanilda, having a bit of fun, pounded the doctor with her fists!

Coppélius was startled. What could be wrong? He rushed back to the book for more information, and Swanilda ran right to Franz and shook him.

"Franz!" she whispered hurriedly. "Franz, please wake up!"

Coppélius turned a page; Swanilda quickly returned to her spot.

"This is it!" the old man shouted. "One last bit of energy! This must bring her to life, or else. . . ." His voice trailed off.

This time, as he waved the final dose of "life force," Swanilda relaxed. Her motions softened, and the mechanical gestures of a doll disappeared.

She stared at Coppélius, and took a step backward, frightened. "Who are you?" she asked.

He bowed deeply and kissed her hand. "I am the one who makes you live." He brought her a mirror. Swanilda pretended to see herself for the very first time.

But then she got to thinking, What fun to start some trouble. Old Doctor Coppélius will be sorry he ever brought *this* doll to life! She began skipping around the room, touching everything that was precious to Coppélius. Delicate bottles, dolls . . . then Franz.

"Is he a doll, too?" she asked. "Let's make him real!" And she started to shake him.

"I cannot do that!" cried Coppélius.

Swanilda snatched the warrior doll's sword and began to duel.

"Stop, Coppélia! Please!" begged Coppélius.

Swanilda began to feel a little sorry for the old man. She stopped, and Coppélius tried to catch his breath. I must find something to keep her from that boy, he thought.

"Won't you dance for me, Coppélia?" he asked.

So she did. With a rose and a fan, she performed a fiery Spanish dance. Then, wrapped in a kilt, she did a fast jig.

When she had finished, she threw her kilt to the floor. She was tired of dancing, and so determined to wake Franz that she tore through the room, bumping into things and setting every doll in motion. Each time she got near Franz, she shook him. Finally, Coppélius caught her. He set her in the chair and pushed her back to the balcony kicking and fighting. He simply had to get that boy out of there, for he would be the ruin of Coppélia!

"Go! Get out! I don't need you anymore!" He pulled Franz to his feet. Franz's eyes were half closed, and he stumbled.

At that moment Swanilda flew into the room again!

"Coppélia!" shouted the doctor. "Get back on the balcony!"

"I am not your Coppélia!" she yelled, throwing off her doll's wig. "*Here*

is Coppélia!" She raced to the balcony, parted the curtains one more time, and dragged out Coppélia's limp doll body.

Franz, wide awake by now, started to laugh. "It's a doll! Oh, I was such a fool!" He swooped Swanilda off her feet and carried her out of the workroom.

And poor old Coppélius was left to weep over his broken doll.

* * *

The next day dawned bright and beautiful, a perfect wedding day. In the square, the villagers cheerfully awaited the arrival of the new bell. The lord of the manor stood there, holding bags of gold for all the newly married couples.

Franz and Swanilda approached the lord to receive their wedding gift.

"Stop!" Doctor Coppélius ran up. "They destroyed my dolls!" he cried. "All the work I've done for years. They must pay!"

Swanilda was truly ashamed of the mess they had made of his workroom. Hanging her head, she offered Coppélius her purse filled with gold.

But the lord of the manor reminded her that the gold was to celebrate their marriage. He pulled out another purse, and handed it to Coppélius. There were hundreds of coins inside! Coppélius accepted the purse and turned to go back in his house, but Swanilda's friends came along and took his arm.

"Come!" One of them smiled into the old man's eyes. "Come enjoy the holiday with us!"

Needless to say, Doctor Coppélius was flattered. The girls led him to a seat and charmed him no end—even more than his dolls had!

Swanilda and Franz led everyone in a joyful, winding dance all through the town.

And the celebration continued until the sky grew dark.

Swan Lake

I'D ALWAYS WANTED to dance *Swan Lake* because, to me, there's nothing more wonderful than to transform yourself into a bird! There's something about the grace of movement in the back, the arms, and the head that lends itself to the characterization.

The well-known version of *Swan Lake* that we see today is actually the second production of the ballet: The first version, with different choreography and at least one third of the music altered, had been a failure.

Marius Petipa, who, with his assistant Lev Ivanov, revived *Swan Lake* in 1895, was one of ballet's most brilliant choreographers. He was born in Marseilles, France, in 1822, but worked at the Maryinsky Theatre in St. Petersburg (now called Leningrad), Russia. Peter Tchaikovsky, who wrote the scores for *Swan Lake, Sleeping Beauty,* and *The Nutcracker,* is now regarded as the first great composer of ballet music.

For a ballerina, *Swan Lake* is a special challenge because she dances two very different characters: Odette, the gentle white swan, and Odile, the beautiful and evil black swan. I love the contrast between these two roles—but I especially enjoyed dancing Odile! There's nothing nicer than to play villains!

LONG AGO AND FAR AWAY, there lived a handsome prince named Siegfried. He was a kind and generous prince, beloved by all his subjects. But as he grew older, the queen grew more and more worried, for Siegfried did not seem interested in ruling the kingdom. Instead, he would go hunting with his friends, or dancing at royal balls.

On the occasion of Siegfried's twenty-first birthday, hundreds of people, both peasants and courtiers, filled the castle gardens for a big celebration. There was a great deal of eating and drinking, and the prince danced happily with everyone. But the high-spirited party suddenly grew quiet when the queen entered the garden.

She was a stately woman, unsmiling, and for her son she had a quite serious message. Soon he would be king, and all his subjects would depend on him. A king should—indeed *must*—have a wife. Therefore, it was time for him to marry.

Marry? The prospect profoundly disturbed the prince.

The queen understood her young son's fears, but she chose not to address them, for she knew he had no choice but to do his duty. "Tomorrow," she said, "six lovely princesses will come to a grand ball at the castle. You will choose one for a wife."

The prince nodded, obedient but brooding. He must have a wife, this he well knew. But tomorrow seemed so soon!

Then the queen turned away, and took something from one of her attendants. "This is for your birthday, dear Siegfried," she said.

Siegfried gasped. It was a stunning crossbow, made of smooth dark wood and carved to perfection. Never had he seen such a bow!

He knelt and kissed his mother's hands. She touched his shoulder gently for a moment, then she turned and swept out, followed by all her handmaidens and attendants.

Siegfried was admiring the bow, when all at once he was distracted by the sound of fluttering wings overhead. A flock of wild swans swooped across the sky. The prince clutched the crossbow tightly and called to his friends. A hunting party was promptly arranged.

While the others moved quickly through the woods in pursuit of the swans, a melancholy Siegfried fell behind. By and by, he approached a magnificent lake. It was wide and dark and curvy, surrounded on all sides by high jagged cliffs. A strange and gloomy castle loomed above, half hidden by a swirl of black clouds. The prince shivered.

Then a most extraordinary thing happened. A swan soared into the clearing—a swan with a gold crown upon her head! Her feathers were pure white, like new snow, and her flight across the sky was dazzling. The prince was struck by her exquisite features. He hid behind a tree to watch her in secret.

There, before his eyes, the graceful swan changed into the most beautiful woman he had ever seen.

He could not help but rush forward. She was terribly frightened and raised a delicate arm in the manner of a timid bird, as if to shield herself from danger. Pointing to his crossbow, she cowered and trembled with fear.

The prince understood at once and placed the bow on the ground. He swore not to hurt her. Then, looking deep into her eyes, he said, "Moments ago you were a swan, and now, a woman. Please, tell me who you are?"

"I am Odette, Queen of the Swans," she began. "I was a princess once, but the evil magician, Rothbart, cast a spell on me. Except between midnight and dawn, I am a swan."

Odette turned sadly towards the lake. "That lake is made up of my mother's tears. She used to meet me here every evening. But in the morning, when I was changed into a swan again, she would cry and cry . . . until finally she died of grief."

The prince fell to his knees, vowing to break the spell, and to kill Rothbart if need be.

Suddenly the Swan Queen shuddered, for Rothbart called. How she longed to stay with the prince, with whom she had fallen in love! But Rothbart's power pulled Odette to him. In a moment, she was gone.

Poor Siegfried. His heart was breaking, for he, too, had fallen deeply and forever in love.

Moments later he heard a soft pounding. The sound grew louder and louder. It was the beating of a hundred wings. Fifty young maidens wearing white-feathered dresses ran into the clearing. They huddled in fear, as the prince's friends had given chase, not realizing that these were girls—not swans—under Rothbart's wicked spell.

The Swan Queen hurled herself between the hunters and the enchanted princesses, and begged the hunters not to shoot. The prince immediately ordered the hunters to put down their bows, and they obeyed him. Odette bowed gracefully, thankfully, then once again she vanished.

Siegfried searched for her frantically among the swan maidens, and when at last they parted, Odette seemed to glide towards him. He took her hand. "How can I set you free?" he pleaded. "There must be a way!"

"If you swear eternal love to me, and if you are true to your vow, this wickedness will end. But if you prove false"—and here Odette trembled—"I will be a swan forever!"

"I swear!" the prince cried out. "I swear eternal love!"

At that moment thunder crashed overhead. Streaks of lightning shot through the sky. And the ugliest of men, in a flowing black cape, stood atop the craggy

cliff, laughing maliciously. This, then, was Rothbart. "You will never defeat me!" he shrieked.

Siegfried reached immediately for his bow, but Odette threw herself between him and Rothbart. "If you kill him, I'll never be saved!" she cried.

So Siegfried could do nothing except watch, helpless and despairing, as Odette began to lose her human form. And while Rothbart cackled horrifically, the swan with the golden crown drifted away.

* * *

The ballroom was aglow with crystal chandeliers. Baskets of rare orchids and long-stemmed roses drenched the room with their sweet scent. Soldiers in starched uniforms lined the hall. The air was filled with expectation, for on this day Prince Siegfried would choose his bride.

Six beautiful princesses flowed into the room, each confident the prince would choose her. How could they know he was thinking not of them, but of the Swan Queen he had met the day before?

The queen prompted her son to dance. So he danced, briefly, dutifully, with each lovely girl. Poor things! He cared for none of them, and dreamed only of Odette. When the queen asked which princess pleased him, Siegfried answered honestly: none of them did.

Suddenly, with a flash of fire, Rothbart burst into the room. A beautiful maiden, smiling, glittering, dressed all in black, was at his side. The Prince rejoiced, for here was his beloved Swan Queen.

Siegfried and Odile danced. Odile was stunning, captivating. So arrogant and proud. The Prince was infatuated. And yet, there was something not quite right. Was it that cold flash in her eyes, or perhaps the way she held her head? Ah, but Siegfried was spellbound, truly blinded by love.

"This is the princess I shall marry." The prince made the announcement to his mother and the court. And the queen reluctantly gave her blessing, for she knew her son would have no other.

Rothbart came forward. How sinister he was! "First," he demanded, "you must swear eternal love to this woman. Do you?"

The prince hesitated, but only for a moment. The instant he raised his hand in the vow, bitter laughter filled the great hall. A ball of fire exploded around Rothbart and Odile.

"Fool!" screamed Rothbart. "Did you think I would let you have Odette so easily!" With a swirl of his cape, he gestured to the window. It was then that Siegfried realized what he had done.

The real Odette hovered just outside the window. She wept pathetically, with all her heart.

Alas! The woman Siegfried had just sworn to marry was not the Swan Queen at all, but Rothbart's daughter, Odile. Rothbart had worked his evil magic to make her look just like Odette. Now the prince had broken his promise never to love another, and Odette would remain under the spell forever!

Stunned, the prince turned and looked again at Odile. An odious expression of triumph and cruelty twisted her features and destroyed her beauty. Siegfried hid his face so as not to see her. How could he ever have thought this was his precious Odette?

Rothbart laughed again. "You have lost!" he shrieked. And with another burst of fire, he was gone. Gone, too, was Odile—and the image of his beloved Odette.

The queen fainted. Siegfried pressed her hand tightly to his cheek, asking pardon. Then he fled from the castle to find Odette.

* * *

The prince raced into the forest, towards the lake where he first met his love. There stood Rothbart high on the cliff, proud and victorious, stirring up a great storm with his powerful magic. Below, the frightened swan maidens huddled against the wind and the icy sheets of rain. Prince Siegfried burst through the group, pushing them apart as he searched among them for their

queen. At last he found her. Odette! He fell to his knees, begging forgiveness.

"I will not go on like this!" cried Odette. "I cannot live under Rothbart's power!" She looked deeply into the water, which was swirling higher each moment. "This lake was made by my mother's tears . . . now it will be my home forever."

"I will die with you!" swore the prince.

Together they ran to the banks of the lake. As they were about to enter the whirling waters, Rothbart's piercing shriek broke through the storm.

"Look what you've done!" he wailed. "You have destroyed me!"

Odette and Siegfried, together, had broken the spell. The power of their love was too strong for Rothbart, and he was dying. The stones of his castle crumbled and smashed to the ground. Rothbart's body faded into the mist. He was gone, forever gone.

The storm was over.

The swan maidens were free.

As the dawn broke, a small boat in the shape of a swan floated towards the lovers, and the prince and his lovely Swan Queen sailed away. They lived together in peace and happiness the rest of their days.

The Nutcracker

The Nutcracker is the ballet I danced the longest, and I never grew tired of dancing it—with its feeling of family, Christmas, and celebration, it was always like a piece of happiness.

Also, I have a particular affection for *The Nutcracker* because of the fantastic music by Peter Tchaikovsky.

I performed in several different versions, and danced the Sugar Plum Fairy, Dew Drop, and the Snow Queen. I never danced Clara, however, because there was no full-length *Nutcracker* being performed in France when I was a child.

Based on Alexandre Dumas's version of E.T.A. Hoffmann's *The Nutcracker and the King of Mice,* the ballet was begun by Marius Petipa. But when he became ill, his assistant, Lev Ivanov, took over. Surprisingly, although the ballet is one of the most popular ballets today, when it premiered on December 17, 1892, it was not an immediate success. All that remains of the original choreography is the final *pas de deux* between the Sugar Plum Fairy and her cavalier.

IT WAS Christmas Eve.

The streets were filled with children, laughing and playing. There was a great deal of squealing, too, as snowballs flew across darkening skies. Such excitement! People rushing home, night rushing in. Carriages scooting by, stacked to overflowing with splendid-looking packages. The cold nipped at passersby, and a blustery wind crackled the night air.

On one of these windy streets stood the Stahlbaum home. It was a lovely old house, with lots of windows upstairs and down. On this night candles burned in those windows, and a large holly wreath hung upon the door.

Now, Clara Stahlbaum and her young brother, Fritz, were not outside playing in the snow, or shopping, or sleighing. They were waiting. Waiting and waiting, just outside the parlor door. Their parents had warned them not to come in until everything was ready!

Each year it was the same, and the children longed to know what mysteries took place in that closed room.

Clara peered through the keyhole, trying to see.

"Let me look!" Fritz pushed her aside.

"No! I was first!" Clara pushed back.

They wore fine, new Christmas clothes. Clara's dress was blue taffeta, with white-lace pantaloons underneath. Her shoes were shiny patent leather, and she felt, if the truth be told, like a little lady. But poor Fritz! He wasn't happy at all, stuffed into a suit that was just like his father's, altogether brown with a jacket of velvet, and a starched white shirt with scalloped edges at the collar.

On the other side of the door, the grown-ups were busy preparing for a big Christmas party. What fussing! There was Mrs. Stahlbaum, topping the tree with a silken angel, and Mr. Stahlbaum, spryly wrapping the last of the presents. And the housemaids were scuttling about with bowls of sweets, and lighting candles, one by one, until the room was all aglow.

At long last the parlor doors swung open.

Clara and Fritz raced inside.

Now what could be more gorgeous than this Christmas parlor? That fabulous glow drenching the room . . . the grandfather clock ticking off in a corner . . . snowflakes that clung to the big bay windows, forming lacy patterns on the glass . . . the roaring fire in the fireplace. In the center of it all towered an enormous Christmas tree, with long strings of popcorn and tinsel, ornaments and candles.

Fritz headed right for the tree, of course, to scoop up one of the presents. "This is mine!" he cried. "I hope it's the tin soldiers I asked for!"

But Clara just stood there, her eyes wide, gazing at the parlor. What magic had been at work, she wondered, transforming the room from its everyday drabness into something so special? The elegant decorations, rich colors, and scents . . . Clara was simply spellbound. Why, the lights on the tree, even *they* were winking, promising some rare enchantment on this Christmas Eve.

The doorbell rang. The first guests had arrived!

Children poured in, their faces bright with cold and excitement. They jumped up and down when they saw the tree and the presents underneath. Like Clara and Fritz, they were all dressed up in their new Christmas clothes. The girls showed off their bell-shaped dresses. And those boys—weren't they handsome in such fancy suits!

Ah yes, it was time to open the gifts! *Oohs* and *aahs* echoed through the room as children plucked toys from their boxes.

When every last present had been opened and properly admired, Mr. and Mrs. Stahlbaum organized a dance. Each mother took her son by the hand; each father took his daughter.

"I do not want to dance!" Fritz sulked. "I want to play with my soldiers! Last year I did not have to dance!"

"You are old enough to join us now." Mrs. Stahlbaum took him firmly by the hand. "You can return to your toys later."

Clara made a face at Fritz as he took his place in the line of dancers. He, in turn, tried to trip her, but Clara stepped neatly out of the way.

"I'll get you later," he grumbled.

The grown-ups demonstrated the steps, and the children, quite suddenly the most perfect little ladies and gentlemen, followed. Then the adults stepped aside and clapped out the rhythm while the children danced alone. At first they paraded slowly, bowing and curtsying to each other. As the music sped up, the boys held onto the girls' hands, and everyone spun wildly.

All at once, the dancing stopped.

A strange dark shadow fell across the room.

Herr Drosselmeyer!

A few of the children stepped back nervously. The boldest ones, more curious than frightened, moved a little closer though, for a better look. Was this a man, or perhaps a sorcerer? Certainly he was odd to look at, with that long black cape and the patch covering one eye. He stooped a bit, too, and leaned across a crooked cane.

Well! Clara went straightaway to hug Herr Drosselmeyer, for he was her dear, dear godfather. He told the most extraordinary stories and, in fact, everything he touched somehow turned to magic. Now that he had arrived, Clara's parlor was even more fantastic than before.

"Merry Christmas, my dear!" Drosselmeyer admired Clara. "You've grown so tall, and what a pretty young lady you've become!"

She blushed.

Drosselmeyer rumpled Fritz's hair and greeted their parents. Then he turned to the group of children. "Would you like to see some magic?" he asked.

Would they indeed!

Drosselmeyer signaled the servants to bring two large boxes.

The first contained a life-sized toy soldier. The other held two more life-sized dolls, a boy and a girl, dressed in the wildest colors.

Drosselmeyer walked to the back of the soldier. Suddenly it leapt stiffly into the air, swishing its sword back and forth! Fritz quickly grabbed his own toy sword and pretended this was his battle.

Afterwards, Drosselmeyer made the boy and girl doll dance a little duet. The children were delighted.

"Come here," Drosselmeyer called to Clara. "I have something for you."

She watched eagerly as her godfather unwrapped a funny little soldier. It was made of wood. This soldier wore a red and blue uniform. His hair was all white, and so was his beard. Clara's eyes widened, for she was used to sweet baby dolls, never dolls like this.

Drosselmeyer reached into his pocket and pulled out a chestnut. He popped it into the soldier's mouth, and pushed a lever. "It's a nutcracker!" he cried.

He started cracking nuts, one after the other, and the children scrambled to get them. Then he handed the soldier to Clara. "Be careful," he warned. "It is very fragile."

Clara gently took the nutcracker and cradled it in her arms. Despite its ugly little face, she already loved it dearly—more than all the other Christmas dolls—because this one had come from Drosselmeyer.

Well, Fritz was rather jealous. Why couldn't Drosselmeyer have been *his* godfather? He always had special gifts for Clara, and this one was a soldier; it should belong to him! "Let me have it!" He snapped up the toy, took the biggest nut he could find, pushed it in the nutcracker's mouth, and slammed the jaw shut.

Clara tried to grab it from her brother, but she was too late. The wooden doll cracked, and its jaw fell heavily to the floor.

She snatched the nutcracker and picked up the broken piece, sobbing as if her heart would break. How could Fritz have been so cruel? And look, he wasn't even sorry!

Drosselmeyer put his arm around Clara. "Let's put it together again," he said kindly. "Have you got a handkerchief?"

So she made a sling and whispered soft, comforting words in her nutcracker's ear. And her nutcracker answered. Clara was sure of it. The other girls gathered around, quietly rocking their own dolls and humming a lullabye—until Fritz and the other boys, blowing toy trumpets and brandishing toy swords, smashed through the circle. What troublemakers they were! Their parents had to pull them away.

"Time for bed," ordered Mr. Stahlbaum and he carried a furious Fritz from the room.

The party was over. Parents bundled up their children once more, and the children made sure not a single Christmas toy got left behind. Hugs and farewells were exchanged with the Stahlbaums. Housemaids blew out the last of the candles.

A quiet settled over the house.

The tree, which alone remained lit, filled the empty parlor with its beauty.

Shhhh! Listen to the quiet.

But what was this? A cloaked figure creeping in . . . Drosselmeyer!

He searched the room until he spotted a toy bed beneath the tree. On top of it lay the broken nutcracker, which Clara had lovingly tucked in for the night.

Drosselmeyer reached for it. A few twists here, a touch of glue there, then he pushed the lever. "Good as new." He smiled, laying the nutcracker back in its bed.

He had just left the room when a small girl could be seen tiptoeing down the stairs. It was Clara. She shivered in her nightgown and appeared rather nervous. So many shadows! Shadows and shadows. Why was she sneaking through the night to the parlor? To be with her poor, injured nutcracker, that is why.

She took it from the bed and, to her great and utter surprise, its jaw had healed!

"But how?" she asked herself again and again. She had no answer, though, and curling up on the couch with her doll, she fell fast asleep.

Bong! Bong! Bong!

Clara's eyes flew open as the clock tolled the hour.

She gasped. Someone was sitting on top of the clock—someone who looked like Drosselmeyer, flapping his arms like the wings of a bat!

She rubbed her eyes and looked again. This time she saw nothing at all. "More shadows," she worried.

By now every dark corner frightened her more than ever. She must return to her own room, and the precious nutcracker must return to its own bed. *Scratch. Scratch. Scratch.* A mouse ran across the floor!

Clara squealed and jumped on the couch again.

The lights on the Christmas tree were suddenly flashing. On and off. Off then on. Clara watched, altogether amazed, as the tree grew and grew and grew . . . until it burst through the ceiling! She truly believed that she, Clara, had willed it to grow, that all the excitement of the evening had forced her world to become bigger than usual. Looking around, she saw that everything else had turned large, too: Fritz's tin soldiers, neatly lined up as if for battle; the toy bed; and best of all, the nutcracker!

Scratch. Scratch. Louder this time.

Oh, no! An army of giant mice crowded the room!

Clara tried to run away, but she could not escape. There were so many . . . they danced around her, baring ugly mice teeth. What nasty grins! Clara huddled in a ball and buried her face in her hands.

Then a trumpet's call, and the thump of marching boots. She looked up. The tin soldiers had come to life! And the nutcracker, too! He marched ahead, leading them into war.

A fierce battled raged. Tin soldiers with shiny bayonets charged the mice. The toy cannon fired the candy cannonballs Clara was collecting off the tree. Trumpets sounded the call to action again and again.

The mice, unharmed but frightened, were about to retreat, when who should appear but the Mouse King.

Now, this Mouse King was twice as big as all the others and terrible to look at. He had seven heads! Each was topped with a tiny crown. Everyone fell

back except the nutcracker. He raised his sword, and he and the Mouse King faced each other.

They began to fight.

With one strong thrust, the Mouse King knocked the nutcracker's sword from his hand. The Mouse King was ready to cast the final blow, and he laughed from each of his seven ugly heads.

Clara had to save her nutcracker!

Desperately she grabbed her slipper and flung it at the Mouse King with all her might. Whack! The slipper hit its mark. What a surprise for the Mouse King. He turned around, sneering at Clara. Closer and closer he came, waving his weapon at her. But the nutcracker quickly seized his fallen sword and stabbed him.

The Mouse King stiffened, then toppled. Holding his wound, he turned and tossed on the ground until, with a quiver, he died.

And poor little Clara, who had never experienced anything such as this, fainted across the bed.

High-pitched squeaks shattered the silence. The rest of the mice scurried left and right, crashing into each other in their confusion and fright. The nutcracker bent over the Mouse King and took one of the crowns. Two mice angrily grabbed the body and carried it out.

Now the nutcracker approached the bed. He waved his arms.

The room melted away as the bed floated into the frosty night.

The cold air woke Clara.

"Thank you!" The nutcracker bowed. "Without your help, the Mouse King surely would have killed me."

He gave her his hand and, as he did so, his nutcracker clothes and mask fell away. A handsome young prince stood in his place!

Clara looked down, suddenly quite shy. She had felt so comfortable with her funny nutcracker, but this boy, this fairy-tale prince, what could she say to him?

And now, with a prince's smile, he took the crown that had belonged to the Mouse King and placed it on Clara's head!

Snow began to fall. Soft flurries danced around them. Then a gust of wind whipped up spirals, forming a curtain so thick that Clara and the prince could not see through it. Drifts of snow turned the world so suddenly and so strangely silent, and an icy whiteness gleamed in the blue-black night.

"Come," coaxed the prince, "we have to find a way out of this storm."

They walked and walked. After a time the snow became gentler, then stopped. The sky grew lighter and lighter. Soon Clara and the prince knew they had arrived in a land unlike any they had known before. In front of them,

chocolates hung from cotton-candy trees. Gumdrops grew like wildflowers. Walnut-shell boats with mint-leaf sails went gliding down rivers of syrup. There was a palace, too, in the shape of a candy box.

"Welcome to the Land of Sweets. I am the Sugar Plum Fairy," a most beautiful woman greeted them at the palace. Her gown was satin dusted with powdered sugar. Her jewels were made of sugar, too, hardened into glistening crystals. Shiny pink slippers graced her feet.

Clara was enchanted. She could not take her eyes off the Sugar Plum Fairy.

"We come from far away," the prince was saying, and he told the story of the war against the mice and how Clara had saved his life.

As he spoke, people made of all different kinds of candy and spices came closer. They were chocolate and peppermint, coffee and tea, marzipan and ginger! When the prince finished his tale, they all applauded.

"You were very brave." The Sugar Plum Fairy took Clara's hand. She pressed it tightly. "We would like to honor you."

And so Clara and the prince were led to a gorgeous table where gingerbread angels set platters of sweets before them, and seated them on a throne made for two.

This was fantastic!

While they feasted, chocolates blazed through a Spanish dance filled with fiery, deep back bends, and clicking castanets. Candy canes leapt through striped hoops, barely touching the ground. Chinese tea popped out of a box in wide split-jumps, while his two helpers fluttered colorful fans. Delicate marzipan shepherdesses held their crooks and danced daintily to the sound of shepherds' pipes and flutes. Mother Ginger wore a wide, wide skirt, and her children ran out from beneath it, scattering everywhere. Clara laughed as Mother tried to catch them! Then flowers made of candied violets and rose petals, led by a joyful lemon dewdrop, blossomed into a whirling waltz. They reminded Clara of her garden in the early days of spring.

The Sugar Plum Fairy and her dashing cavalier danced an elegant duet. He took her hand, and she balanced on the tips of her toes. They spun and glided across the floor. The dance finished as the Sugar Plum Fairy plunged daringly into his arms. He lifted her triumphantly.

Clara was so enthralled she forgot the delicious chocolates in front of her. Someday, she thought, I will dance like that, and she stole a glance at the prince beside her.

It was time to go.

A little reindeer-drawn sleigh would carry her home. All the candies gathered round as Clara and the prince stepped inside. They waved and waved as the sleigh flew through the air.

"Merry Christmas," whispered Clara.

And the Land of Sweets vanished in the distance.

Giselle

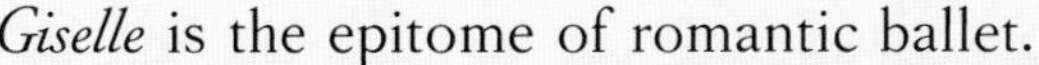

Giselle is the epitome of romantic ballet.

What ballerina wouldn't want to dance *Giselle*? It is for her what *Hamlet* is for an actor. I worked on *Giselle* and lived with it all my life, but, unfortunately, I danced only a few performances of it.

The idea for *Giselle* began when a French author named Théophile Gautier read a book on German mythology. He was particularly fascinated by a myth about creatures called "Wilis," and thought it would make a pretty ballet. Within three days, Gautier, along with author Vernoy St. Georges, had written the story for *Giselle;* and within one week, composer Adolphe Adam had finished the score!

Jean Coralli choreographed the ballet, along with Jules Perrot, who staged Giselle's solo dances. It premiered in 1841.

Giselle is a ballet, not only about the love of two people for each other, but about the love of dance. It is dance that unites Albrecht and Giselle, and is the basis of their romance.

A ballerina named Carlotta Grisi was the lucky dancer who first danced this difficult role, which demands both brilliant technique, and acting.

LONG AGO, in a small village tucked away in a forest, lived a lovely peasant girl. Her name was Giselle and, more than anything, she loved to dance.

Giselle's mother was in a constant state of worry, for her daughter was not very strong. "Remember what can happen to girls who dance too much," she cautioned again and again. "You don't want to become a Wili."

Wilis were the spirits of young girls who died of broken hearts. Each evening they arose from the mist in wispy-white dresses to dance. Should a man come along and cross their path, these wicked spirits would surround him and force the poor fellow to dance . . . and dance . . . and dance . . . until, completely exhausted, he would drop to the ground and die. All the villagers feared them; any young girl who loved to dance too much was warned to take care.

But sweet Giselle just could not stop dancing.

Now Giselle had a sweetheart whom she loved with all her heart. She called him Loys; but in fact, Loys was really Count Albrecht, just pretending to be a peasant. He had spotted Giselle and had instantly fallen in love with her. So he had come, not too long before, to live in a cottage near Giselle and her mother.

Early one morning, Count Albrecht swept into the little village. He could not wait to see his darling Giselle. How he adored her! So how could Giselle ever imagine that her beloved Albrecht was—oh, pity!—engaged to someone else, someone considered more suitable for a count?

Albrecht knocked on Giselle's door. Then he hid, for he loved just to watch her.

"Hello?" Giselle stepped outside and looked around. She saw no one. Puzzled, she turned to go back in. But Albrecht's cottage caught her eye and she stopped.

"What would I do if he were here?" she wondered, and began to do a little dance. "I would bow to him this way." She curtsied daintily, then frowned. "No, no, I would bow this way." She tried again. Still, she was not pleased. She shut her eyes, to picture Albrecht's face. "Oh, this would be right." And with that, she curtsied deeply and gracefully.

Albrecht was delighted. He moved quietly toward Giselle. She, so involved with her little dance, did not even notice—until she bumped right into him!

Giselle was so embarrassed. She lowered her gaze, too shy even to look at him. When Albrecht took her hand, she pulled away and tried to run back to her house. He caught up to her though, and led her to a small bench beside his cottage.

She sat, spreading her skirts over the bench.

"Perhaps you could leave a little room for me?" he teased.

She blushed and moved over—but just a bit. Albrecht sat very close. Giselle slid further away! He moved closer again. This time she jumped up!

"Wait!" he called.

Giselle paused.

"I love you!" Albrecht raised his finger in a vow. "I swear it, Giselle!"

"No! Do not swear; it is bad luck." Giselle reached for a daisy. "This will tell me if you really love me." She pulled off one petal. "He loves me."

Albrecht smiled.

Giselle plucked another petal. "He loves me not." Oh, sadness! She quickly counted the rest. "He loves me not!" By now, utterly miserable, she flung the daisy to the ground.

But Albrecht took it up. Furtively, he pulled off a petal. "You made a mistake," he said. "Look—he loves me, he loves me not, he loves me!"

With that, he tossed the flower in the air, and taking Giselle's arm, they started to dance. Someone was watching them, though. It was Giselle's neighbor, Hilarion, desperately jealous because he, too, was in love with her.

Unaware of the intruder they danced on, Giselle playfully leaping out of Albrecht's grasp again and again until, finally, he caught her and kissed her firmly on the lips.

"Stop!" Hilarion dashed forward and pushed them apart.

"We were just dancing," Giselle said meekly.

"Just dancing?" Hilarion laughed in an ugly way. "I saw you, Giselle, kissing him!"

"Leave her alone," demanded Albrecht.

"This is none of your business, stranger." Hilarion shoved him harshly.

Angrily, Albrecht reached for his sword, and found it wasn't there. Too late he remembered that he had removed it, for only a nobleman wore a weapon at his waist. Nobody here in the village was supposed to know his true identity—and especially not this nasty Hilarion.

Just then a group of villagers came by to celebrate harvesting time. They surrounded Giselle and insisted she join in. So she grabbed Albrecht and started to dance, laughing and spinning, blowing kisses in his direction. What fun she had! Until—with a sudden short cry—she began to sway. Had Albrecht not been there to catch her, she would surely have fallen.

In a few moments Giselle was fine again.

She stood up, although rather shakily. "Let's dance some more!" And despite Albrecht's concern, she started in again.

"Stop, child!" It was Berthe, Giselle's mother. "What are you doing?"

"Dancing." Giselle stared at the ground.

"Haven't I told you over and over, it is very dangerous for you to dance? When I think of all those tales about the Wilis. . . ."

"No, Mother! Please don't say that!" begged Giselle.

"There are men who have gone into the forest and never returned! Young girls who died unhappily and whose souls never found peace! Giselle, you must listen to me." Berthe pulled Giselle from her beloved Albrecht, and marched her straight to their cottage. What else could Berthe do?

Albrecht and the other villagers slowly returned to the fields to continue harvesting. When they had gone, Hilarion sneaked into Albrecht's cottage. "I must find out," he murmured, "who this stranger really is."

Meanwhile, a hunting party from a nearby castle was just stopping in the village for some refreshment. Their arrival created a flurry of excitement, and before long, Giselle and her mother had set up tables and were serving food and wine to the noblepeople.

Among the party was an exquisite lady named Bathilde. Giselle knelt beside her, and touched her gorgeous dress, smoothing it against her cheek. How could sweet Giselle possibly know she was the very woman to whom Albrecht was engaged to marry!

Bathilde turned, surprised. "What is your name?" She spoke gently and with grace.

Giselle flushed and backed away.

"Do not be afraid," coaxed Bathilde. "Now tell me, what is your name?"

"Giselle. I live in that cottage. I sew and weave, but most of all, I love to dance."

Bathilde smiled. She liked Giselle. "Do you have a boyfriend?" she teased.

"Oh, yes!" Giselle smiled widely. "Soon we will be married!"

"I, too!" exclaimed Bathilde. "Well now, you said you love to dance. Do you think you could dance for me?"

Giselle's mother started to protest, but a villager reminded her that if a countess wanted Giselle to dance, then dance she must.

Bathilde looked on with pleasure as Giselle performed a small dance filled with delicate steps and soft jumps, arms curving above her head like a halo. When it was over, Bathilde removed her own necklace and slipped it on the young girl's neck.

Giselle was thrilled! Bathilde was, too—in a more genteel fashion—for there was much in the giving that pleased her.

And off they went to Giselle's cottage so the countess could rest.

Soon the harvesters returned, carrying armloads and bushels of grapes. Albrecht held a wreath to crown the Queen of the Harvest. This year the villagers had chosen Giselle!

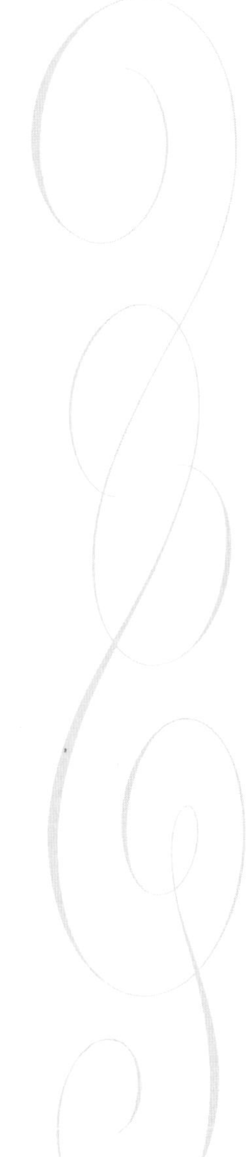

"Giselle!" they called. "Giselle! Giselle!" When she came out, they lifted her onto a cart wrapped with grapevines and luscious flowers. "Dance for us! Dance for us!"

"May I?" This time Giselle asked her mother.

"No! No! No!"

"Please! Mother, please!"

Reluctantly, her mother agreed.

Giselle flew into a dance. Her legs traced little circles in the air. She twirled faster and faster, ending in a sudden graceful pose. The she grabbed Albrecht's hand.

"No!" Hilarion rushed over, forcing them apart. He shook Giselle by the shoulders. "You think he loves you! Can't you see he's not like us?" He thrust Albrecht's sword at Giselle. He had taken it, and a hunting horn, from Albrecht's cottage. "This belongs to him! A nobleman's sword!"

Wide-eyed, Giselle backed into Albrecht's arms.

But Hilarion kept on. "He's lying about who he is!" he told the villagers. "We don't have swords like this."

Albrecht was in a rage. He snatched his sword from Hilarion, and would have killed him, had two peasants not held him back.

Then Hilarion blew the horn and the hunting party poured out of Giselle's home.

"Albrecht!" Bathilde rushed over. "What are you doing dressed like . . . like a *peasant*?"

Albrecht could not answer. As if he were sleepwalking, he took Bathilde's hand and kissed it.

Giselle threw herself between them. "Albrecht?" she cried. "His name is Loys and he is going to marry me!"

Now Bathilde was truly surprised. "This is Count Albrecht," she said patiently. "He is engaged to me, my dear. He could never marry a peasant."

Giselle grew pale, for one look at Albrecht's face told her that Bathilde did not lie.

With a scream, she ripped off the necklace and tumbled into her mother's arms.

Then a dreadful thing happened. Giselle flung back her head. She rose, stumbled, and laughed the joyless laugh of a madwoman. Wandering through the crowd, she bumped into one person and nearly fell into another, recognizing no one.

And slowly, she began to dance. This was a remembering dance, and in it she repeated everything that had happened that day. She bowed to Albrecht's cottage. She moved towards the pot of daisies and plucked one. "He loves me, he loves me not. . . ." She could not go on. The daisy fell from her hand, and her body crumpled.

Alas! With shocking speed, she pounced on Albrecht's sword and would have stabbed herself to death, had he not grabbed it from her. Giselle looked at him in horror, then turned away. Then she danced as she had once danced with Albrecht. Her slow, dreamy steps grew wilder and wilder, until she could no longer take the strain. Bent over in pain, tears streamed down her face.

"My hands — so cold." Giselle shivered uncontrollably. Her fingers fluttered up and down her arms. She gazed upward and, with shaking hands, pointed to something only she could see. "How pretty they are in their long white dresses," she whispered.

"The Wilis!" Giselle's mother was distraught. "She sees the Wilis!"

Giselle dashed through the crowd once again. Hilarion stopped her. "Go to your mother," he pleaded. "Go to your mother!"

Giselle ran to her mother and hugged her.

Then she broke away and cried, "Loys!"

Albrecht reached for her, but Giselle slipped away.

She was dead.

* * *

Hilarion knelt at Giselle's grave, deep in the forest that surrounded the village. Tenderly, he made a cross with two pieces of wood. The light began to fade and he worked faster, for he knew the dangers that lurked in the forest at night.

As he set the cross on the grave, he thought he saw something move. And again . . . it was pale and barely visible, like a mist. Hilarion said a prayer quickly and hurried away.

A ghostly figure dressed in white, with a tattered veil across her face, floated into the clearing. It was Myrtha, Queen of the Wilis. She removed her veil and danced weightlessly towards a myrtle tree, from which she broke two branches. Then, skimming over the ground with airy, flying leaps, she tossed one branch left and the other right.

"Wilis!" she called. "It is night—our time to rule!"

The Wilis came, each wearing a white wedding dress just like their queen's.

"Dance!" said the queen.

So these girls, who had loved to dance—and died dancing—danced once again. They moved towards each other, crossing the clearing with little hops.

"Tonight another shall join our sisterhood," announced Myrtha, moving

towards Giselle's grave. "Arise!" She lifted a branch and Giselle appeared. Again Myrtha waved the branch. Giselle came closer. Her veil was whipped off, and she whirled and leapt across the clearing.

Myrtha waved and the Wilis scattered.

Just then Albrecht came along, wrapped in a long cape and carrying a bouquet of lilies. He tumbled to his knees at Giselle's grave and buried his face in his hands, for Albrecht was filled with grief.

Giselle stepped lightly beside him. He raised his head, puzzled. He felt that something had come near, yet he could not see anything. Giselle moved in front of him and he lunged forward to touch her, but she was too quick and his arms circled only emptiness.

"Giselle," he prayed, "please come back."

And so she came, dancing around and above him, showering him with lilies.

But now the Wilis were returning!

Giselle whirled and flew away, with Albrecht in pursuit.

The Wilis dragged in a frightened Hilarion and threw him at Myrtha's feet.

"Dance him to death!" she ordered.

"Someone have pity!" Hilarion ran down the line of Wilis, begging for help.

"No. No. No." Every girl refused him.

And one by one they flew at Hilarion, pushing him to dance. His steps grew heavy and tired; still, they would not let him stop.

Finally they circled Hilarion and herded him over to the nearby lake. A slight shove and he toppled over the edge.

The Wilis were victorious.

But there was more to do. Albrecht was next!

Giselle pleaded for her lover, but Myrtha simply turned away.

The cross at her grave . . . there was protection! Giselle led Albrecht to it, and stood in front of him, her arms outstretched.

Myrtha approached threateningly, then suddenly she shuddered, for this cross had powers that were stronger than her own. But more than fearful, she was crafty. "Dance, Giselle. Dance as you never have before." And this cruel queen watched, triumphant, as Giselle's graceful movements drew Albrecht from the safety of the cross.

Giselle and Albrecht danced together, quietly and gently, expressing their love for each other.

"Continue!" demanded Myrtha when they stopped.

Giselle danced alone, imploring her love to rest. But Albrecht could not keep from joining her, and they flew into a bright and wild duet. This was a stunning performance, with Giselle soaring over the ground. In the end Albrecht caught her and lifted the featherlike Wili high above him.

"And now," screamed Myrtha, "he shall dance alone!"

Hypnotic music drove him faster and faster; Albrecht wanted to stop but he could not! He stumbled, then he fell. Giselle ran to him and caressed him with her cool soft hands. His eyes remained shut and he breathed heavily.

"Please!" begged Giselle. "He is too weak to dance any more. Please let him live!"

"He must dance until he is dead!" cried Myrtha. "We Wilis have no mercy."

So Albrecht danced again. How weary he was!

Giselle longed for just a glimmer of the morning light, for then the Wilis would melt away in the mist, and her beloved would at last be free.

"Just a little longer," she whispered. "Soon it will be morning. . ."

Albrecht forced himself to go on but, in truth, he could barely move. "I cannot. . ." He fainted on the spot.

Just then bells rang out—morning bells! Giselle gratefully lifted her arms in prayer, as Myrtha and the other Wilis faded . . . faded . . .

She cradled her Albrecht, and gently rocked him. But now she, too, was

fading. And, showering him with the last of the lilies, Giselle disappeared forever.

Albrecht stared into the empty space where only moments before his beloved had danced. Then he gathered the scattered lilies and placed them back at her grave. Wrapping himself up in his cloak, he took one last glance at the clearing and left, freed by the grace of Giselle's love and forgiveness.

Sleeping Beauty

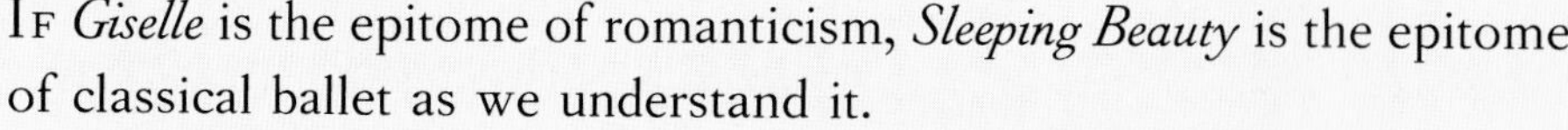

IF *Giselle* is the epitome of romanticism, *Sleeping Beauty* is the epitome of classical ballet as we understand it.

The role of Aurora requires harmony, balance, and good taste — the qualities you need to be what we call a prima ballerina. From the innocent, happy sixteen-year-old, to the young woman in Florimund's vision, to the maturity of marriage, it's a role that passes through three stages of life and that you have to build.

Based on the fairy tale by Charles Perrault, *Sleeping Beauty* is another collaboration between Marius Petipa and Peter Tchaikovsky. It premiered on January 15, 1890. It was received rather coolly at the time, but is now a favorite with ballet goers, and regarded as the test of a ballet company's classical ability.

Once upon a time there lived a king and a queen who were exceedingly happy, except for one thing. They longed for a child.

After many years their dream came true. The queen gave birth to a lovely baby girl. They named her Aurora, and their joy filled the land.

There would be a christening, of course. And a grand party which, by royal decree, was to be the most splendid occasion the kingdom had ever seen. The preparations began at once, for everything must be perfect.

The finest seamstresses were called in. They worked night and day embroidering delicate lacework for the christening gown. Solid gold dishes would adorn the banquet table, and the little princess would be toasted with magnificent gilded goblets. Not one, but two ladies-in-waiting were to sit by her cradle. Then there was the matter of the guest list. The king's attendant, Catalabutte, took great pains over it, for he must not forget anyone—especially the fairies with their magical gifts.

And so, the day of the royal christening arrived at last.

When the king and queen swept into the ballroom, the very best musicians were on hand to play the fanfares. The court bowed down in reverence and the royal couple sat upon thrones of thick soft velvet.

The fairies entered one by one. Now, fairies do not move as humans do, for they are not used to walking slowly upon the earth. Rather, they glide lightly over the ground, seeming almost to fly. In this way the fairies arrived, each paying homage to the king and queen with a gracious curtsy. Altogether, they made a glorious sight in their shimmering dresses of yellow, orange, white, and lilac.

The elegant Fairy of the Crystal Fountain came forth slowly. She waved her long, willowy arms over the baby in a blessing. "She shall be the most beautiful princess that ever lived."

"She will be as sweet as an angel," said the Fairy of the Enchanted Garden, who flew towards the cradle in a series of quick jumps.

The playful Fairy of the Woodland Glades giggled as she announced, "The princess will be graceful in all she does."

"And she will dance beautifully." The Fairy of the Golden Vines, fluttery and birdlike, showed off a few steps herself.

"Princess Aurora will sing like a nightingale," trilled the Fairy of Songbirds, who moved so fast, and changed directions so often, she could hardly be kept in sight.

The Lilac Fairy came last, as she had the most power and deserved the place of honor. She was just approaching the cradle to offer her wish, when a trumpet sounded.

In rushed a page, white with fright. "Carabosse has arrived . . . and we did not invite her!" His voice shook fearfully.

"Carabosse?" Pandemonium filled the ballroom, for Carabosse was, indeed, a most evil fairy. Quite by chance she had been left off the guest list, for it was thought she was dead, or perhaps enchanted.

But alas! She was alive and very angry. She burst into the ballroom in her dragon chariot, attended by ugly rat servants.

"A grand banquet for the new princess," she cackled, "and I, the most powerful fairy of them all, not invited! How could this be?"

The king and queen and the ladies-in-waiting tried desperately to shield the baby in her cradle, for Carabosse was in a terrible rage. Courtiers cowered. Guests scattered. But no one could hide from Carabosse.

"What fool forgot to invite me?" she roared, pointing a gnarled finger at the queen. "Was it you?"

Then she pointed to the king. "Or was it you?"

She tore around the room. "Or you, or you, or you?"

The king trembled. The queen asked for pardon. The other fairies surrounded Carabosse and pleaded with her to have mercy. She only mocked them though, and would not be quieted.

"Who was it?" she bellowed. *"Who forgot me?"*

The terrified king pointed to Catalabutte, who knelt and begged forgiveness. But the wicked fairy threatened him with her walking stick. She snatched his wig from his head, tossing it to her sharp-toothed rats.

Then Carabosse swept across the room to the cradle where baby Aurora slept. "What a lovely child!" she sneered. "Well, I have a wish for her, too! When she is sixteen, she will prick her finger on a spindle and she will die!"

As she spoke, her creatures pranced about, laughing.

The court flew into an uproar.

But there was one who remained calm: the Lilac Fairy.

"I have not yet given my wish," she announced, stepping forward. "It is true that I haven't the power to undo all that my elder, Carabosse, has done. But I can do something. Instead of dying when she pricks her finger, Aurora will sleep for one hundred years. Then a prince will come and awaken her."

At each word that the Lilac Fairy spoke, Carabosse seemed to shrink a little more. Furious at being overruled, she jumped back on her chariot, whipped her fire-snorting dragons, and drove off into the black night.

"No!" stormed the king. "I will not allow this spell to come true." He turned towards the court and decreed, "From this day forth, any person in this kingdom found spinning, or even owning a spindle, will be put to death!"

The very next morning, the king's attendants went from cottage to cottage until there were no more spindles in the land.

* * *

And so the years passed happily. Princess Aurora grew into a charming, graceful girl.

Then her sixteenth birthday arrived. The time had come for her to marry, and the king and queen invited four of the most handsome, kindest princes to a grand ball so that Aurora might choose the one she liked best for her husband.

The ballroom was indeed sumptuous. Colorful bouquets of flowers sweetened the room and made it festive. Courtiers waltzed holding garlands, and children carried little baskets of posies and carnations.

Princess Aurora was radiant as she danced into the room. She hugged her parents, for she loved them dearly. They led her to the four princes. She lowered her eyes and curtsied demurely, and each prince handed her a long-stemmed red rose.

Now at first, Aurora had felt shy. But as she held the flowers to her cheek, and saw the princes gaze tenderly at her, she decided that she liked the attention. She became more and more joyful, and flung her roses into the air, showering the king and queen with the fragrant flowers.

She is radiant, thought the first prince.

I hope she will marry *me,* thought another.

She is the most beautiful princess I have ever seen. The third prince was enchanted.

I have never before danced with anyone so lovely. The fourth prince wished his dance would never end.

Just then an old woman walked into the ballroom. She stood off to the side, holding a colorful bouquet.

"Oh, how very pretty!" The princess ran over and sniffed the flowers.

"They are yours, my lady." The old woman bowed.

"Thank you." Aurora smiled graciously.

Quite suddenly though, she cried out in pain and dropped the flowers.

The king and queen rushed over.

"What is it?" cried the queen.

"I've just pricked my finger on a thorn," said Aurora. "It's nothing." But she stumbled slightly, and her face grew very pale.

The princes all tried to help, but Aurora pulled away. "Please do not worry. I am fine." She tried to join in the dancing, but grew dizzier and dizzier. Spinning crazily, she lost her balance and fell!

The king grabbed the bouquet the old woman had given his precious

daughter. Ripping apart the flowers, he discovered a spindle hidden in the blossoms.

A hideous laugh rang through the ballroom. The old woman whipped off her cloak—it was Carabosse!

"My spell has come true!" she shrieked. "Aurora is dead!"

At that moment the Lilac Fairy glided in.

"Take the princess to her bed," she commanded. Then she turned to Carabosse. "Leave at once. Your spell has failed, for she is only asleep."

The court, made brave by the lovely fairy, echoed her words.

And Carabosse slunk from the room.

So Aurora rested on the softest blankets embroidered with gold and silver. The tearful queen bent to kiss her, and listened for the princess's gentle breathing.

The Lilac Fairy waved her wand, and the entire court fell asleep, just where they stood. Darkness settled over the kingdom, and thick sharp brambles encircled the castle so that no one could get in to harm the sleeping princess.

* * *

And so, Aurora slept for one hundred years.

One day, when it was nearly time for her to wake, a handsome young prince named Florimund happened to be hunting near the castle. By now, the tangled branches hid the building entirely, and everyone had forgotten the vanished kingdom.

"We will stop here to rest," the prince announced to his party. He was feeling terribly sad, although he knew not why.

The servants prepared a meal and, when it was over, the prince's friends played blindman's buff. They danced and listened to music. Beautiful women, fashionably dressed, hovered nearby, wanting to be the prince's partner. But somehow, his mind was far away.

"You are very quiet today, Prince Florimund," one of the party remarked.

The prince merely smiled. "All this company tires me a bit. Why don't you go on? I shall rest here and join you in a while."

In fact, for reasons he himself could not understand, the prince had no intention of joining them. When everyone had gone, he wandered over to a nearby lakeside. Leaning against a tree, the prince gazed off into the distance. There was a queer feeling inside him. Was it sadness or something else perhaps?

All at once, the Lilac Fairy stood before him. The prince knew from the suddenness of her appearance and the strangeness of her dress that this was no ordinary human. He bowed to her immediately and asked, "Who are you?"

"I am the Lilac Fairy." Her voice was smooth and gracious. She pointed towards the forest. "Deep inside those tangled vines lies a castle. Do you know about it?" she asked.

Prince Florimund did not.

"There lies an enchanted princess who has slept for one hundred years. She will continue to sleep," said the fairy, "until a prince wakes her with a kiss."

"Am I that prince?"

"If you wish to be." The fairy smiled. "Would you like to see her?"

The prince would. So the Lilac Fairy waved her wand, bringing forth a vision of Aurora, surrounded by a group of maidens.

Enchanted by Aurora's beauty, the prince ran towards her, but the maidens stopped him. He kept trying to catch her, but could not. He might touch her arm, or raise his hand to her cheek, but he could not hold her.

"You must be patient," warned the Lilac Fairy.

Heeding her words, Prince Florimund knelt quietly.

In time, Aurora came to him. She danced slowly, exquisitely, and each moment that she did so, Florimund fell more and more in love.

But alas! The princess glided away, and she and the other maidens disappeared.

Prince Florimund ran back to the Lilac Fairy. "Please take me to her!" he implored.

The good fairy waved her wand one more time, and a small boat floated

to them. They stepped inside and sailed through the darkest part of the forest, through small openings in the thick vines, until they reached the wall of thorns that protected the castle.

But, miraculously, the curtain of thorny vines parted as they walked forward, until at last they reached the castle door. Through the halls and up the steps they went; through the still and silent castle. All the while, the prince was astonished to see people fallen fast asleep in the middle of their tasks.

And then, quite suddenly, a bright light shone through the darkened palace. They had reached the princess's bedroom.

The prince could not resist bending down and kissing Aurora.

Her eyes opened.

She gazed upon Florimund and fell forever in love.

"Is it you, my prince?" she asked. "I have been waiting so long."

The palace brightened at once, and all the people in it awoke from their hundred-year rest.

Very soon after, the prince and princess were married.

Their wedding was splendid in every way and, once again, joy reigned in the land.

A grand procession of fairy-fale characters arrived to honor Aurora and Florimund. There was Cinderella with her Prince Charming, and Princess Florine

with the Blue Bird, who flew in beside her. Puss in Boots marched past with a pretty white cat. To the court's amusement, they pounced and stalked each other, playfully batting their paws.

Little Red Riding Hood was chased by the wolf! And shiny magical jewels of gold, silver, and diamond came to life and dazzled all the guests with their beauty and dancing.

Finally, led by the Lilac Fairy, all the fairies entered, ready to give their blessings to the handsome couple.

Aurora and Florimund danced a wedding duet. She fell back into his arms as he whirled her around. He lifted his beloved princess high in the air . . . and once again, she dived into his arms.

When the wedding couple had finished, the whole court joined in and danced as well.

As for Carabosse, she was so angry at not getting her way that no one ever saw or heard from her again.

But Aurora and Florimund lived happily ever after.